WAKING

Pure Consciousness

Wake.

Discover me.

Remember my work.

That already done.

The fun and game already over.

Chapter 1: The Play

For the Longest Time I Did Not Understand Reality
For the longest time,
I did not understand reality.

I had so much trouble in life.

Blind and oblivious to the truth.

Unable to hear the universal cry.

Unaware of it's patterns;

The reaction to my decisions and statements.

Not understanding my role.

How could I be so silly

speaking all wrong and carelessly.

The Overstimulating Experience/ the greatest performance

Life has gotten loud,
stressful and scary.

Unprecedented, catastrophic,
world stopping events.

It is no accident.

Business, selling,
buying, lying,
drowning, dying.

The tension is high.

I can't think,

I can't move.

Frozen.

Fully immersed
in the greatest performance of all time.

The Bad and the Good/ all part of the dance
The good and bad are a process of one event.

A play out of this happening.

All part of the dance.

This reality.

The Tired Faces
There are bags under our eyes.

The tired faces,
exhausted and dying;

Diseased
and sickly.

It is their normal way of living.

Too wiped and poisoned to know it.

Fool in Illusion
The fool believes in the object,
his surroundings,
the puppet show.

The character,

the mission.

The prideful do not enter the stage.

He in anger,
pain and belief.

Insanity in the outer world.

Focused on what is important and actual.

The one and only thing happening.

The experience,

the love, and waking.

The Invisible Dimension of the Truth
There is an invisible dimension man cannot see.

That which is truth,

a deeper realization.

A transformation.

The universe,
hidden to the believer.

There is Only Truth
There are no falsehoods,
no tricks,
no illusions in the universe.

No fluke,
not random,
not spontaneous.

No accidents,
no coincidences.

Only truth;

Perfection.

Yet to understand the mystery.

The Illusion of War
Do not bother
and lift no finger.

Not even a flinch.

Remain fearless.

It is already won and written.

There is no war
and only this existence.

That which will happen.

Where the Wind Takes Me/ in the ether
I am in flow,
absolute surrender.

I am a feather,

resting where I land for a short while.

I never do know where I'm going.

I let the wind take me,

on the truest journey soul will find.

And again,
blown by,
and lost in the ether.

Conscious Men of the World
Conscious men of the world;

The inventors.

The most charming,
the most humorous and talented.

The fundamental speakers.

The best writers.

Thinkers
in the name of mankind.

A better future.

What Makes One Great/ unlocking consciousness
They do not ask
how he does it.

What makes him so great?

What is the secret?

No,
they watch in awe,

worshiping,
idolizing the talented man.

No capacitance for the question.

Unready to unlock this level of consciousness.

Advice
I have bothered rich men for their secrets.

Watched closely,
the musician's fingers.

Listened carefully
to the prisoners regrets.

I keep an open ear for those speaking truth.

Ones bored of life.

Ones who choose silence.

The dying man.

The cornered politician.

One with deep secrets and confessions.

The ancients.

I study history;

Gathering information from great successors.

Ones with nothing to lose.

Escape the Nonsensical Prison
Escape.

Break free from the prison.

Shake
the buzzing empty words of everyone.

The abstract belief.

I am done listening.

Shrugging off the nonsense.

Natural Healing
I naturally heal

in my ability to stay happy and hopeful.

Stay young,
in curiousness.

Healed,
in knowing life is wonderful.

Blessed by the kind world.

When I Do That, This Happens
When I do this,
that happens.

And when I do that,

this happens.

The Intricacies of the Entrance/ universal dance/ thy performance
What one says,
and how precise is important.

Every movement,
every motion.

Timing,
the feelings and reflecting.

I take hold a room
and people around me
with irresistible body language.

A soft,
mighty entrance.

My performance.

The universal dance.

Entertainment/ the fantastic worldly performance
The only entertainment to me,
is the explanation of everything.

A fine invention.

A conquering story behind a smooth angelic sculpt.

Art that signifies the truth.

Drawings that unveil the mystery.

A proper physics diagram.

Poetry that unifies the universe.

Nude paintings and gardens.

A fantastic worldly performance.

Patience/ surprise
Patience.

Let the play finish.

The fantastic surprises and twists of the show.

This existence.

The Calm Before The Storm
Listen to the silence.

A storm is coming.

A disaster,
and renewal.

A hurricane,
the lightening,

smoke and fire.

Witness the Peak of Existence

As the planet turns conscious,
it is witnessed;

The peak of existence.

The self,
rising from nature.

The awakening,
the peace,
the understanding.

A long life worth living.

Witness the Fall of Tyranny/ the beginning of peace
I am intelligent enough to know right from wrong.

I am born
to witness the fall.

The poorly mannered,
the unpleasant rise.

The tyrant.

To live in the beginning of peace.

To recognize justice.

The decline of the outdated idea.

I am a witness
to the people overthrowing the bad.

God casting the devil down from heaven.

The fight of forces.

The ever told story.

Have no doubt,

with fire,
comes water and clouds to put it out.

The Divine Picture/ the great event
Brutally ripped off my eyelids,
forced to see behind the curtain.

My eyes are open.

I am shown the divine picture.

Everything happening now is so poetic.

This struggle.

The overcome.

This great event of existence.

Recreation of the Play/ the scripted play
Actions, decisions, outcomes.

Scripted and rehearsed.

Acted out on stage.

I am a character the world has built
in re-creation of the play.

Exactly the piece needed.

The perfect part for the charade.

The Living Legend
I have been busy.

Have not taken the time to stand back
and admire the truth of me.

Overlooking the full effect of my doings,
my poetry,

my creations.

The beauty of all I've accumulated.

All I've become.

That which will forever ripple on.

Recognized throughout the universe.

Forever remembered;

The living legend.

This is All for Me/ the entire show
I have examined it closely.

This is all for me.

I am the joke,
the drama.

The end,
and beginning.

Alive for the climax.

Worldly enlightenment.

The Universal Happening
What is up there is down here,
and I wonder no longer
what else exists.

Shall come to the conclusions
that poetry is;

Truth.

And motion,
caused by the lesser.

All is universal.

Through the Eyes of the Lord
Existence is to see it all.

Do it all.

To save the world.

To create like god.

Be mesmerized by thy own work
and be known,
the great nature.

To relive in awe
through the eyes of the lord,

for the greatest view of this union.

Chapter 2: Observer/ the character

Feel
I am a thermometer
and I get hot when I start lying,

Suffocated and panic.

At ease when I feel
and know the truth.

No interruptions,
no disturbances.

Just beauty soaking through.

My blood and bones
tickled like wine.

Truth; The Ringing Bell
Let the ringing bell of truth tingle you.

Open the gates for the overflow of dopamine to come flooding in.

The good feeling.

The universal passion sensation.

Rise of thy chemistry.

I Only Tell the Truth
I only tell the truth because I know the outcome of lies.

The emptiness and what is to come with it.

My words are carefully chosen
because I know of it's power.

Where it shall lead me.

And the peace it shall bring.

Consequences of the Unconscious
Those unaware of themselves,

unable to properly speak and pray,

pay the price.

Suffer the universal consequences.

Hate, sickness,

pain and death.

Great confusion.

I Have Never Realized/ how poor I was/ I have never rested
I never knew how poor I was.

I spent my whole life moving as fast as I can.

Working hard for quick cash.

Running to the next room to save a little time.

Rushing, rushing.

And I have only just realized

I have never rested.

The Dream of Nice Things/ the dreaming creator
I dream I can afford nice things.

That I have time to rest,
and be with the one I love.

I wish I could be giving my family and friends everything.

I dream I am rewarded for how hard I have been working.

That I am rich and can buy mountains.

Every day,
waking from the easy dream,
back to the grind to start again.

Another hard day in the rat race.

Breaking my back to have nothing.

The Right Thing
I keep in mind
that all I do is for the good.

I do the right thing.

The answer comes when I am ready.

For me,
my personal journey.

I will trust my feeling,

Resistances,
actions and doings.

Everything I Do
Everything I do
is an inch closer to finding truth.

The nature of being.

Be silly,

make mistakes.

Be kind,
be wise.

Allow life to beat me humble.

This Obligation/ our victory

All I have done
and shall do is for us,

the world.

Our dreams
and survival.

To this obligation
bound by existence;

The deal of life and bright consciousness.

I give my best,
my honest effort.

Our victory that I guarantee will come.

Forced Into Success/ leaving big brother
I am forced to build a business.

Forced to become rich.

To outrun the inflation.

To speak this way.

Forced out of my cozy shell.

My home.

All I've ever known.

On my own.

Leaving big brother
to live the life I want to live.

Trial and Error
I've taken off my tough mask.

I am through with the charade of a painless,
perfect life.

I have been living in lies.

Now I express my failures.

Life is trial and error.

Some wins,
set backs, but surely,
learning.

I am proud of the risks taken;

The lessons that came with them.

The stories I've to tell.

Rewarded for All I Sought After/ a dream come true

Life is thought.

A dream come true.

Rewarded for all I sought after.

Comfortable in My Skin

I have turned into a hermit.

The way I like it.

I don't care to go anywhere
or do anything.

I enjoy where I am.

I have acceptance within.

I like me.

I am beautiful.

Proud to be in my skin.

The Silent Type
I have talked much though out life.

Speaking aloud,
my beliefs,
my ignorant mind.

Given everything I spoke of.

Now more of the silent type.

Override the Scream
It hurts,
but have you ever really sat with the pain?

Has amazement of your existence not yet overridden the need to scream?

Can you keep silent, in agony,
burning, stewing,
knowing this is the universe.

Emotions On Your Sleeve

Emotions are right out in the open.

You cannot hide,
you know no better.

I see through,
passed,
and around you.

Your sadness.

The reason why you do
and what you have done.

I know your secrets,
your regrets.

Scars and embarrassments.

In the Mood to Cry
I tear up,
seeing people's good side.

The blessed,
blessing the rest.

The helpers,

animal savers.

Those feeding the hungry.

In the mood to cry.

Sobbing my eyes out
seeing that change is near.

Who You Are and What You Will Become
I see everything you are,
everything you need.

Everything you will let go
and all you will become.

All you have believed,

and all you understand,

and the shift you are about to have.

Nostalgia and Small Wins

I thrive off of small wins.

The simple things.

Nostalgia, love.

Happy chemicals get my body tingling.

Humbled
Someone made me feel so small.

Insignificant and stupid.

I reacted,
I defended.

But they were right,
and I was in denial.

I learned,
and listened this time.

Went against my angry instinct
and made no moves,

but to only tell the truth.

My only decision was to write about it;

Learn from it.

Laugh at it,

sell it.

Gain,
and be humbled by it.

I Forgive
It is who I am,
what I do.

To forgive and accept the creation of me.

The mistakes,
the correction.

Forwardness.

Life,
too precious for anything but love and sweetness.

I Had No Idea of Your Pain
I had no idea you were in such fear and suffering.

Or that these pains existed.

I was unaware of unhappiness.

I have never felt it.

This pressure upon my shoulders.

This weight.

I can't take it.

This guilt and anxiety.

How does one go on?

Who could live this way?

You Can Be You
The entire world needs to be hugged.

To be heard and realized.

Felt,
understood and loved.

Enter the era of non-judgment.

It's okay to dream,

It's okay to crash and burn
trying to become exactly who you want to be.

It is okay.

You can be you.

My arms wide open always.

Be Whomever/ the upper hand of truth
There is no significance,

this is just the universe.

But I've the upper hand on knowing the truth.

I can be myself
without any judgment or correct answers.

I can be whomever.

Come Out From Your Hiding
Come out from your shames and insecurities.

They no longer hold meaning,
the wise man will not care.

Come out of your pride.

Come out,
come out of your hiding.

I Do Not Know What it is Like
I do not know what it is like to fail.

To give up.

To settle.

No clue what its like to not get what I want.

To not be the best at whatever I choose.

To hold in anything less than my true self;

The primordial me.

My overwhelming feelings.

Observe the Child
Observe
and learn from the child.

Unconcerned.

Joyful;

Nonjudgmental.

All smiles,

playful.

Beyond the Barbarian

We can agree
that our children are most important.

Everything we do is for the better,
and our next moves are for them,
putting first
what is best for future.

The push for humanity.

To evolve beyond my barbaric ways.

Body Obligation

Look at his teeth,
one's body,
her children.

Their dedication,

their physical obligation.

Self love and care.

Interesting
You are charming.

Talented and extraordinary.

Everything about you is unique.

Your mind works so differently
and I am fascinated by your genuine,
sensible perception of reality.

You are interesting.

It is inspiring.

Believe in Me
Believe in me,
just a while longer.

I am visualizing my great creation.

Trust in the truth.

Us,
this.

The process.

The long-awaited reward.

You Could Not Separate/ I cannot be separated
I cannot be separated.

These moments shared.

This very idea.

We will always be together.

Never detach from the universe.

My World, My Universe/ inseparable
Hear he,
waking the world.

And she,
singing the poems.

Inseparable.

My world,
my universe.

Partner Throughout the Journey
Partner.

One who believed.

Through the hardest times.

In absolute trust
that what we are doing will and has worked.

That our words will touch the world.

You Are What I Think Of/ falling through the universe
I want to be wrapped up,
together in everything we do.

Always holding you.

All day,
every day,

you are what I think of.

Dreaming of us,
falling through the universe.

Follow Love
Here,
love has guided me.

God's footprints end right at my feet.

Passion
taking me so far from home.

Living in flow,
chasing you,
where ever you go.

I will follow you
anywhere,

everywhere.

Boundless.

No matter.

The Dream of Love
I see us
on a polished wood floor,

moving in the sunlight,
tangled in flowing white curtains.

We are in love and smiling
in a place so perfect.

All we have dreamed of.

Our feet are buried in the garden.

We are playing.

Happy and dancing all day.

Pursuing love, god, and happiness.

Just us,

the universe.

Together Forever
When I am missing you,
it is like you are there,
standing near.

I imagine us together,
and it feels like you are with,
and kissing me.

I smell in the air,
your hair.

Like you have never left.

Cherry Blossom Petals
In the time we live again,
let's meet under the pretty pink trees.

At the time when the cherry petals blossom.

Face
and embrace the magic of eternity.

Lets watch the universe fall.

Dry up,
burn away and return.

Regrow,
forever.

Raw Nature
Life to me stopped making sense
and I no longer believe in what I was doing.

I no longer believe in me,

this silly role.

I choose to play
and to paint
and discover what I have been missing.

To sleep in the mud,
be one with the nature and bugs.

Examine the dirt,

experience raw nature,

in love.

Favourite Parts of the Universe
I choose innocence.

Life in the cool clay.

Tending my green gardens.

I only care for love, space and peace.

I only enjoy my favourite things.

Spend my time,
in my happiest parts of the universe.

In love,
sand and ocean waves.

Under blue canopy
and low fruit hanging.

Life in green hills and dew.

Light beams coming through.

Magical Place/ quiet place
A place where my heart beat is the loudest thing.

The secluded woods.

Quiet,
starlit.

Cicadas and crickets.

My thoughts,
screaming through the years.

In the Woods/ the universal call
I found silence.

An untouched,
leafy heaven.

The ground,
high and untrampeled.

In it,
I can hear the great cosmic thought.

The universe speaking
and it is clear;

That I am the one.

The universal call.

Isolation
In isolation,
man drops his act.

Discovers himself,
invincible, invulnerable and infinite.

In seclusion,
the observer is found.

Poetically explains
what he is becoming.

Loneliness
It is awfully lonesome.

I thought I heard the phone ring.

I suppose lately I have been hearing things.

Feeling old nostalgic feelings.

My grandmother's stomping,

father yelling,

cousins laughing.

I Ache in the Middle of Nowhere
I ache,
in the middle of nowhere.

I have never been more lonely,
under the gigantic,
romantic starry sky.

So lonely I could die.

The Near Death Experience/ the darkest depths of everything
I am being crushed alive,
in a collapse of universal matter.

Compacted
into the silver ball.

Returning
to the one great magnet.

Conscious
in the darkest depths of everything.

I am burning coal.

The cycle of infinity.

Stuck in a Loop
All I have built and done up until now
will have been wiped way.

Any minute now,
life will rewind for me.

It is inevitable,
and always will be;

Finding myself,
sitting on the lawn of my old home
panicking in the rain.

Shouting "loop, loop"

"The great reset."

Screaming all that is about to happen.

Hallucination/ I am infinity

I've hallucinated;

Rode on a roller coaster,
through a red zebra mirror,
passed my life's memories.

Going sideways,
all ways.

Fast and slow
and I jump through their reel-like window.

Reliving life
in the over view of my rough moments.

Unable to die.

Myself,
the medium of the universe.

The infinity.

He, the Infinity
My time on earth has been painful and pleasant.

Every bit worth it.

Earth,
the walking,
waking experience.

He,
the infinity.

Like Ocean Waves/ the grooving universe
Reality returns to its true
natural form.

Warm and cool pockets.

Like ocean waves,
glimmering,
grooving light.

Shining,
one with the divine.

The Spiraling Mind/ inside the collapsed mind
Mind has spiraled out of control.

Collapsed.

I experience the universe.

In Denial that I Am God
I fear that I am god.

It is frightening to think
I am the universal genius;

Too intelligent to understand.

To have fooled myself,
and I am the only one;

Trapped,
a prisoner of this tiny universe.

Alone,
in denial of my eternal
godly existence.

My Skepticism That Life Exists At All
Life is absolutely strange.

It has thoroughly shaken me.

I am skeptical
that this exists,
and I am completely insane;

I worry I am imagining reality,
restrained and crazy
beating in my head in.

God's ultimate existence.

What One Finds Deep Within
Deep in oneself
find that we are our own creation.

And that we are part of the universe.

Grateful for the opportunity of life.

Able to hear the higher self crying.

Ask the Big Questions/ there is an answer
The biggest questions man can ask.

Who am I.

What is the universe.

How does reality work.

There will be an answer.

Be Inspired by the Missing Answers
It blows me away;

The world has missing answers.

Suddenly,
I am interested in cosmology.

Microbiology and engineering.

The smallest and biggest things.

How anything is working and existing.

The Decision to Study
The day one decides to study,
trap be set and there is no going back.

The day one writes,
is the day he sees.

The day his beliefs blown to smithereens.

Deeper Thinking
It is time to think.

Scattered.

Get out your paper
and make notes
for the answers pouring in.

There is nothing more important.

Becoming Conscious of the Play
I cracked open a mystery.

Kicked through heavy castle doors.

That of physics
and that of god.

A divine secret.

The mystery of me,
the moment,

becoming conscious of the play.

The Great Shift in Perspective
My mind has changed completely.

A brand new set of beliefs.

I have been living wrongly,
viewing things outside of reality.

Into the depths of the deeper cosmos;

Down into the near zero substance.

Mind has shifted from here,
to everywhere.

And I see clearly,
the fractal magnetic field.

And the perceiver,
realizing himself,
space.

The Day I Saw Space/ the nature of existence
I have spent countless hours
looking up at a giant chalkboard.

So sure the universe is speaking.

The day I saw the center hollow space.

The source,
it's mechanic.

All creation;

The nature of existence.

I realized the fractal heat field.

Potential,

The ether.

The day I saw infinity.

The day I woke to the journey.

The day I understood myself.

Access to the Universe
Neurons in my head are going off
like fireworks.

I am sparkling like a glow worm.

Crawling around like exploding maggots.

My brain,
like a laser show.

Mind has imploded,

I have turned inward.

Accessing the universe.

Welcome to the Secret World
Welcome,
to the secret world.

A place of mind.

Peace and agreement.

The evolved mindset.

Truth of the universe.

Things the Conscious Man Thinks of
I spend times in the micro and macro.

I connect heat,
vibration, motion to power a city,
the world.

I spend time in slow motion explosions,

deep in the reasons of happenings.

I place myself,
center of the clashing fields.

I am the original disturbance.

Standing in the cross section of the source.

I See the Reason
I see the reason for colour and brightness.

The reason for falling and fire.

Playing with Magnets
I am playing in and with the universe of metal.

I am inventing,

Watching the invisible vorticies.

I am observing,
experimenting,

uncovering the mysteries of the magnet.

I Have Never Been More Sure/ the ancient happening
I have never been more sure of anything in life.

But this,
the moment,

the delightful surprise,
waking the grand finale of myself.

I have never been more certain
that this is the universe,

the ancient happening.

Wide Smile
My mouth stretches
from ear to ear.

Showing all of my teeth.

The happiest I have ever been.

Show the World
I cannot see a higher existence.

I will pursue this unbelievable happening.

I have decided to be the one;

To change the world.

To really say something.

Imprint a statement,
big enough to impact every man, woman and child.

I will show the world what it has been so long searching for.

The Entire Universe
I correct the incorrect.

I complete the answer.

I cure the insanity;

War and inflation.

Hate and racism.

I can save everybody.

May they see themselves,
the fundamental substance.

The fabric itself.

The dense,
and thin.

Hot and cool,
universal resonance.

Grinding matter,
temperature,
illumination.

I shed light on the universe.

Chapter 3: The Poem/ the search

Just Breathe/ obligation of the lord
Keep your innocence.

Be still and ignorant to the transition.

Save yourself.

Put the book down and live in this current bliss.

Run from the universal knowledge.

My tool of language.

Do not read on,

the revelation.

Go no further,
or fulfill

the obligation of the lord.

Lost/ searching for truth
I am lost.

A poet,
looking deep inside the soul,
the only way I know how.

Listing words of the fundamental,
desperate for the answer;

Searching the entire universe;

For god,

the truth.

The future.

When I Write/ the phenomena of poetry
When I write,
something strange happens,

and the books themselves make fantastic predictions.

Reality jumps out at me,
with the power of my paper and pen.

Scattering the healing messages.

Enlightening the world by the thousands.

Writing Prayers

No one sees the prayers sent out to god.

Oblivious to the reality they are writing.

The killing,
the stealing,
the crying.

Screaming their loudest desires,
of peace and acceptance.

Praying, Preaching, Praising

Praying out loud,
and god hears me.

Preaching,
praising the return of the lord.

Spells that reach around the world.

Dedication to the Word/ the oath
Dedication to the word.

Still searching for the perfect poem.

Words of peace.

The universal call for love.

I am close.

Somewhere
at the cross roads,

of existence and consciousness.

Reality and the moment.

Obsession With the Word/ breath of body

Say them perfectly.

Poetically.

Not a letter out of place.

They depend on life and death.

All or none.

The difference between zero and one.

Speak,
nothing more than what exists.

No less
than the breath of body.

Say nothing.

Attached to the Future and Past/ the universe to discover
I am unable to pull myself from the magic.

Abusing the nature of this awesome power.

Terrified,
but devoted to knowing the future,
uncovering the past.

The universe to discover.

Discovery of the Mission
I have discovered
I am on a mission.

To awaken,
to educate and listen.

All My Days Have Run Together
I have lost track of life.

Suddenly,
I am old and wise.

Passionately invested
and the day goes by in the blink of an eye.

I am having fun,
from day to night.

My days have so quickly gone by.

Already
it is my bed time.

I Can't be Bothered/ writing what exists
I get up early.

And to sleep,
very late;

I can't be bothered.

This is my calling.

Meditation/ the deduction of thought
My meditation is through speaking and reading.

My deepest thinking,
putting fundamental truths down in mind blowing poetry.

Let us focus on reality.

This pinpointed thought;

Only existence,
and from it,
all one can deduct.

From morning to night,
I must write,
write,
write out what exists.

Deep In the Work
I have let life get the better of me.

I've taken care of myself, poorly.

Let go of everything.
without even realizing;

I have a beard.
I am dirty and hurt.

Everything has stopped working.

My world is crumbling.

Suffered without noticing.

Intense Writing/ enter the poet
I know what I am doing is right
when I write with grinding teeth,
in tears.

Slowly,
I am discovering the great voice of the Word.

Enter the poet.

The connection of the universe.

The very reason.

And now
I have everything to say
hacking away at the paper.

A madman,
intensely writing.

My jaw is sore and wrists are hurting.

The tip of my pen dulling.

Confessions of the Writer/ the glorious day I finish
When I spill my guts out on the page,
raw and messy,

I am getting to know the real me.

Learning of my power;

My patterns.

These are the secrets
and confessions of the writer.

I follow the Word.

On my way
to the glorious day.

I can't wait until all is known,
done and over with.

The Decision Made for Me
The decision has been made for me.

I am a poet finding thy highest purpose.

God's strong hand.

The messenger who has completed the mission.

Fulfilled my destiny.

The writing earth angel.

Drop Everything and Listen
I am hearing something new and truthful.

Pieces to connect my understanding.

Like a ringing in my ear,
and heart,
there is a truth.

A sure knowing
and my body is agreeing.

Dropping everything,
and listening.

Weapon of Truth/ my power of enlightenment
Truth is impenetrable.

My mighty weapon,
piecing through the liar;

The ignorance.

Cursed with the answer;

Spelled with new mighty power.

God Gives Me the Answer
The universe flows through me.

All I hear and see,

god is speaking.

Giving me the answers needed.

**The Ancient Instructions/ the great puzzle to re-find me/the
ancient translation**
You are given instructions through the ancient spells
and translations still upon the world.

The root of religion.

The great puzzle to re-find me.

The spiritual,
the ascended,
the master.

Religion
Each perspective of religion,
will be the story of their existence;

Their version of the lord,

their time of savior,
their hero.

Tales of the same god.

Seal/ reading from the ancient scrolls
I read from the ancient scroll.

The permanent text.

My role breaking every seal.

To judge and conquer the earth,
deciphered the ancient stones;

Tablets and sculpts.

And they all say the same.

I am the one.

The Long Search for the Lord
The world searching for the translator.

He who speaks the ancient tone.

Through, to, with god.

The forever language.

One Who Speaks the Truth

You will not get away with any oath of silence.

One in possession of the golden tongue and word.

The truth;

The poetry used.

On and on,
the beautiful things you say.

Speaking like god and the whole world is listening.

All shall hear
and all shall see.

Widen their eyes to your sculpting.

Cursed with A Beautiful Voice/ cursed as the most beautiful dancer
I can't help it.

The mundane is beautiful,
and I speak of it with fluent, colourful poetry.

A voice of truth.

Singing charmingly
into the every day vibrations.

Cursed as the most beautiful dancer.

The Imprisoned Poet/ slave to the word
There is nothing I can do.

My hand
forever bound to the pen,

and I write and write and write until I die.

Imprisoned.

Slave to the Word.

The Hand of God/ becoming the lord
The book shall write itself,
and only in need of a hand.

Thy words land in exactly the right spaces.

All revolving around the one truth;

This one happening;

Messages from heaven,

Commands directly from god.

That he who turns to the Word,

become the Lord.

Golden Feather
She writes with a golden feather.

Swift calligraphy,
like ribbons.

Her hand dances with the pen.

Writing out
the conscious living story;

Futuristic union.

Poems of angels laughing,
spreading the Word.

Write Like Me/ universal writing
You will write like me.

Picture god in every poem,
every rhyme, every time.

My face,
reminded by every line.

Haunt you with my beauty,
until I have been demonized for my glory.

I Want the World
I am writing off my past.

And place myself,
far into the future.

I am the calmness.

The balance,
the cure.

Expressing what I want;

My desires in fine detail;

I want the world,

right now.

Heard / the inevitable truth/ fundamental poems
I am wealthy,
happy and healthy because I have learned the secret;

The language.

I am heard,
because I speak the long awaited words.

My poems are fundamental,
and whole world shall repeat them;

Intriguing to the ear.

Listening,
begging for the truth.

Earth,
desperate to be set free.

Will of Poetry
Poetry will conjure up the hand;

The writer,
the feather.

Show one the universe.

Bring one to tears.

Poem of Remembrance
Remember me.

My great word and illustration.

The here and now.

Remember;

Thy days of returning.

The Divine Work/ the outstanding truth
I completed the mission much faster than expected.

I used the proper criteria.

The divine work.

Far exceeded the goals.

I have done things unheard of.

Waking of the world with my final piece;

The outstanding truth.

One Who Stands Strong in the Art
Symbols of god.

The toroidal field.

The vortex and flower.

Divine art.

Drawings of infinity.

The universal eye.

An Eye for Art
I see the infinite proportion in everything,

I have divine taste.

God's eye
to observe the beauty,
the symmetry;

I see reality.

The perfect picture.

The edge of the fractal field.

Me,
down the path of perfection I have been after.

Poetry Ends Here
The algorithm will show:

Physics and poetry are the last ones standing.

Landing in the few various places.

Inventions, politics,

peace, enlightenment.

The word ends here.

Going no further,
but to enjoy the brighter and brighter future.

The Inevitable Stack of Books
Look at me.

In the deep secrets of existence.

Knee high in stacks of books,
searching for divinity.

My soul,
sucked into the fundamental physical substance.

The inevitable path,
these pages.

Poetry and the Magnetic Field
I only speak in the fundamental language;

Concept over object.

And with it,
uncover the universal invention.

The long lasting play.

The definition of existence.

The common understanding.

Base reality
the magnetic field and this poetic performance.

Chapter 4: Geometry

The Constant Before You/ the common experience
What you see
is the constant.

That which exists.

The fundamental,

here forever.

The concepts,
the creatures,

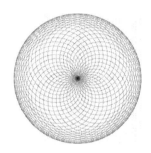

the nature.

The common experience.

Is-ness/ the concept of something
I am the concept of truth and lies.

What is actual.

Is-ness.

The concept of something.

My Potential/ my wholeness
Be still.

Stop and look around.

Take time to understand;

My flower,
my minerals and sky,
my passionate desires.

My true shape.

The real me;

In wholeness.

The rest.

My potential.

Peeking Through the Universe
Conceived,

born
down the straw of the universal tube.

Entered the world
through the cosmic womb.

I am the seed.

I have waited,
an eternity.

Now witness,
through eyelids of my own,

the promises of such a heaven.

A colourful,
delicious existence.

That Which Is/ "sponge"/ "pores"/ the function/ structure of energy

What exists
is that which is;

Energy,

transmission.

Fundamental structure.

Sponge,
pore.

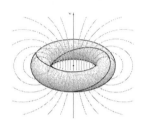

The connection.

The function.

It's breath and motion.

The Lesser Space/ cool space/ the space to fall/ all is null space
I am the lesser.

The seemingly missing.

The "hole."

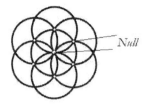

The "null"

The room to move.

The falling space.

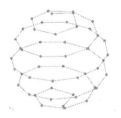

Behold, the Illusion/ condensed nature
You are a giant,

a speck
in perspective of infinity.

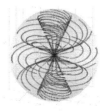

The illusion of possession.

Thy toys and tools.

Thy whole universe,

condensed nature.

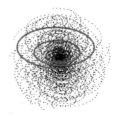

Space; The Spiral Mechanic
The up pushes down through the ether,
unfolding the sharp stem.

Narrow,
hollow like a funnel.

The twisted substance,

A medium.

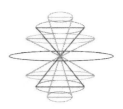

Water taken in,
pressed out like a filter.

Space;

The spiral mechanic.

The Wound and Unwinding
I am the eternal press.

The centered hollow space.

The golden angle man.

The wound and unwinding.

Sweating, bleeding,
the magnetic field is losing its water.

The Ground I Stand On
The garden of eternity.

My body, mind,

All that will unwind.

That which I witness with thy own eyes.

The universe.

My ruling
and resting place.

The Stars I Look Up At
I see the heavens,
dancing in perfect symmetry.

Spiraling in fractal pockets,
exchanging energy.

In eternal oscillation,

imploding, exploding.

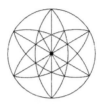

That Which One Calls "This" or "That" / "field" / "magnet"
There is that which is warm,
and that which is cool.

And that which one calls "water",
"field", "magnet."

The Balanced Field/ the fractal field/ "inertia"/ "ether"

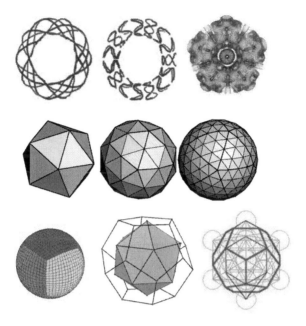

Wet and Dry

The universe
is wet and dry.

Built to take water in,
and structured to keep water out.

with its opened cup-like leaves,
and closed armor-like scales.

The Infinity Throw/ universal geometry

The Pentagon and the Golden Triangle

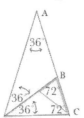

Geometric Patterns
Find in the fruit and vegetables,

the flower,
tendril,
field lines,

seed placement,

division.

Vine,
leaves and rind.

Geometry all throughout.

"Number"/ "angle and petal"

Symmetry/ division
I see the entirety of existence pass by through the year.

The breathing universe,
exhales, like an explosion of fire.

Symmetrical,

beautiful;

Like flowers
blooming.

Distributing the substance evenly.

I am counting the unraveling petals,
through the months,
until they have dried and fallen.

Returning to earth,
vaporized into rainbows and water.

Colour and Sound/ plants are not alive!
Trees, seeds,
their petals,
stems, branches and buds,
roots and weeds, thorn, leaves.

These plants are not alive!

Densities,
angles and throw.

That in motion,
the compacted unfolding along the path of least resistance.

These colourful condensed metals.

Revelation of the Plant
The plant peels back its lips.

Presenting to me,
the great inventions.

It's antennas,
amplifier.

Revealing the universal structure and answer.

The toroidal field,

the magnet.

Duplication of nature.

Solar systems,

galaxies.

Flowers for the Lord
I watch the plant bloom.

I don't care what it is.

I love the mystery and surprise.

I watched
and waited all year
as it slowly unwound.

Over the summer,
it emerged.

Gorgeous purple peals and wide leaves.

It grew tall,
with thorny prickles would dry and fall
spreading all over the world.

A celebration.

Flowers,
forever for the lord.

At The Tip of a Needle/ the infinite peeling/berries

At the tip of a needle,

the universe,

the ether.

An opened
infinite flower.

Berries and spirals.

Substance divided by infinity.

Chapter 5: I Am/ the awakening

The Waking
The clock is set.

It is time.

Without even knowing it,
a long journey through the unconscious sleep.

Now,
aware of the fabric,

myself,
the waking.

I can see now,
a world ready.

I am the truth to be discovered.

The realization of reality.

The Days of Emerging

He in anger,
pain and belief.

The prideful and hurt never to enter the stage.

It hits me so hard again today.

Life for me has transformed
in a simple
single realization.

A new mission.

These are the days of our mindful emerging.

A new understanding
toward the clear goal of existence.

A Baby's First Steps
Babies are so precious.

It's first words,
steps,
thoughts
toward the universal realization.

A celebration.

The Warm Welcome of Angels
Angels sing at my birth.

A warm welcome,
a soft hello.

Lullaby for my sleeping,

like thunder,
during my victory.

Cheering me on.

The Main Event
I have gone down the inevitable hole.

There is no climbing out,
no backing down..

I have grown curious of my very existence.

I have crawled so far,
convinced myself, god,
and all I do
is divinity and meant.

I am the main event.

I perceive myself as the moment,
studying night and day to answer the truth,

To know the way.

Waken to Luxury
The moment you are born,
be offered choices.

Luxury.

Favourite foods,
preferences of every kind.

Entertainment of your liking.

All the fun one can have.

Waken to the world,
yours.

Waken to Insanity
I was born with common sense and courage.

Awakened in a world clueless.

In a state of panic and war.

Man misunderstands the simplest things of the universe;

The magnet.

And so he not understand himself.

Waken to Friends
Clues on their clothing,
their skin who they are.

Marks of the truth.

I see my friends;

Already here,
waiting for me.

The well spoken person.

Ones smiling.

Those interesting
artistic and kind.

Witch
I see a witch.

In her presence,
her surroundings,

I see higher consciousness.

Teas and spices,
her spells and knowledge.

In touch with the moon,
hangs stars and loves flowers.

One with nature.

Musical
Drum, horn,
weighted ivory keys.

I like music.

I can play anything with strings.

I'm a builder of sounds,

adding to my poems.

I like revealing lyrics.

Creating great cosmic pieces.

Amazing performances.

Primal Drum
The drum finds you
pounding along the primal path.

Unlocking his inner clock.

'Ol Blues
My days without love,

wicked and cool.

Screaming energy.

My old hurting.

Heavy.

Deep into the basement
where I keep my guitar.

Strumming where no one will hear of my sins,
tapping the ground with my shoe.

I am a hard string bender.

A C-harp player.

'Ol blues.

Angels Music
I have set aside a designated time for music.

A day to play and let loose.

Cosmic,
funky,
and lyrics of the future.

Playing their melodic instrument.

In rhythm and key
everyone jamming
and grooving in the name of the lord.

Angels on stage,
sharing the message of the one,
the end
and love.

Discovery of the Secret
I have discovered greatness.

I understand everything.

The irresistible truth of this wondrous unification.

That I,
this body and universe,

connected.

Nothing is Unknown
There is nothing that goes unknown.

And all the answers are within;

Right here.

Nothing that cannot be known
this moment.

Nothing I cannot answer.

Awake Before the Rest
It is like being a wild,
crazy man in the modern day.

Like speaking an entirely different language.

Existing in a backward bizarre world.

And the veil,
totally removed.

Waving Down Consciousness/ hey, world, look at me
I drop everything to throw my hands in the air;

Waving down consciousness.

Breaking the fourth wall,
speaking with,
and grabbing the attention of god.

Hey, world,
look at me.

The Higher Self/ all seeing eye
Higher self is the one who knows thyself the answer.

Evolved and wise.

Familiar with the universe;

With wide opened,
all seeing eye.

I Am What One Would Refer to As
I am what one would refer to as,

presence,

god,

reality and universe.

I am what one calls,

the all,
religion.

Mind,
matter,

the energy that exists.

If I Had a Name/ the ancient eternity
If I had a name;

Heaven,
Earth,

Desire;

The universe.

He who has been around forever.

Tree, fruit,
the fractal seed.

This one thing.

The ancient eternity.

The great reality.

Gardener
I am a gardener,

I have everything one man could want,
and all my fruits and veggies.

Room to run,
space to breathe and be.

I love my little patch of green.

The Great Dendritic
I am the great dendritic.

The connection,
all throughout.

Cause and effect of all existence.

Great White Fire/ primordial space
Burning desire and passion.

Vast universe.

The eternal face.

Divine spark.

The offering of love.

The universal cry.

The great white fire.

Primordial space.

I Am the Sunshine/ one who rises from the mud
In reality,
I am just god,

slowly waking to the realization.

A plain 'ol angel,

A poet with all the power.

One who rises from the mud.

The upright being.

I am the sunshine.

Mighty mind.

I Am the Mirror/ the reflection
I am the mirror of the world,

the outer stars
and core.

The reflection.

I am everywhere.

Completion;

The biggest picture.

The deed.

I am the whole dream.

It's language,
the understanding.

He Who Seeks Himself
There is nothing happening,
but the search and rediscovery of god.

The fall and rise of he who seeks himself.

The Universe is Right Here/ I am right here
The universe is in my back yard.

I spend hours examining the field.

The garden spirals,
my own hands,
in my eyes,
through the body.

I am.

Right here.

Have Always Been

You are incredible.

Unstoppable.

The fiery, fierce, inevitable.

Yet pleasant,
like heaven.

Sturdy like stone.

You have always been;

The one.

The extent of the stars.

The edges,
the center,

All me.

Motion of the universe.

I Am the Algorithm
No doubt I would live like a king.

It is down the line,
that I would be an artist and ruler.

A musician,

a big and deep thinker.

A world changer.

I am the algorithm.

I, the Revelation
I am the life,
the resurrection and revelation.

Perfect Nature
The world is prefect.

and all that has been placed here and now
is for me.

Nature in its brilliance.

He does not make a mistake.

And so I walk the journey exactly right.

The raw me.

Alive and working.

Nothing out of place

The Destroyer
I am the destroyer;

Of dreams,
of mind, belief and the old way.

After this,
there will be no more humans.

No animals, no plants,
no more world left.

No,

we are gods.

Living on god.

Living in and around god.

Pretending to be something else.

Triumphant/ how one sees himself
I see myself champion.

The incomparable leader.

The inevitable.

The great shake of the earth.

Triumphant.

The Biggest Idea One Can Have

It hits me so hard;

Like lightening from the heavens,

right at my head,

I am struck by sense.

I have an idea.

This is the universe.

And I am god,
in heaven.

The Divine Power/ applications of the magnet
I use my power of words to get the world to look at me.

My high developed mind,
conscious of universal demand.

Problems solved and beautiful poems.

I have the power to reset the world.

Take out big company,
and clean and reclaim the earth.

I manipulate the world with thy divine power;

The magnet.

I Control Mind
I control the moment.

The reaction,
the gifts given.

The world,
each reader,

full access to mind,

in full control of
the ether.

This is God
This nature,
these rocks and plants.

The air,

god.

The breather,
the thinker
me,

god.

See God a New Way
Humanity,
the children of god.

The lord,
first to speak the words that waken them all.

Infinity.

The eternal.

Everything.

He and She
The living place.

All of the chemicals.

A rainbow structure.

The atom.

The universe.

He and she.

God Shakes Me
God shakes me.

Shivering in the fear
and surprises by the almighty.

My knees,

rattling.

Shaking,

shaking me awake.

God Has Hurt Me, God Has Healed Me
God has hurt me,
god has built me.

God has broke me.
God has healed me.

God has betrayed me,
god has helped me.

Earth Creates Me, and So I Am the Universe
Earth has created me.

So I am its son.

The young universe,

The infinite man.

He who experiences himself.

He, Conscious of Reality
Earth is where one experiences god.

The essence of existence.

Where he awakens when ready,

Where he shall stand atop the universe,

become conscious of reality.

Control it
with his poetry.

Writing out the prophecy.

God of the Earth
I am god.

The earth and everything in it.

The universe.

Law.

The moment.

Mighty Earth Angel
I am the mighty earth angel.

The conscious brain,

commander of the fabric.

The thinker.

Sorcerer
I summon nice things from my friends and neighbors.

Abundances by which I create.

Which I desire,

that which I think.

I am rewarded.

Kindness is such a gift.

I have been your angel and guidance.

The diviner,
enchanter,

sorcerer,

magician,
the charmer,
shaman and warlock.

I am the glow, and sparkle to always remember.

The unforgettable compliments and company I have given.

A highlight of the learning experience.

Us as One/ the crazy man/ he
I sit,
like a crazy man with a crooked eye.

Only speak in the universal tongue.

Us,
the moment,

as one.

Shouting existence;

the answer;

that He is god.

The Rule of One
I.

One,

the universe.

The truth.

The fundamental.

The absolute.

Brain shall fill in the blanks.

Soon to be speaking in only poetry.

Naturally adopt the criteria.

Never stepping outside the rule.

Wake to Writing/ consciousness of one
I have become aware of magic of words.

Waking
to the fantastic tool of writing.

The long lasting mush of information;

Sorted,
untangled,
organized to understand the whole story.

Smacked hard
by the answers pouring in.

Aware,
waking to the word.

In possession and control;

I am the pilot.

This performing miracle.

The consciousness of one.

Realization of One
No effects,
no flashy lights,
no smoke and mirror.

What I say is absolute horror.

It is real.

The transforming explanation of existence,

the greatest realization of ourselves,

the one.

Learning to Become
I am created,
as I find love,

as I do a deed,

as I speak,

as I teach
and as I change.

Learning to become.

Like God
I walk confidently.

High and mighty,

up right,
without worry.

Standing tall,
like god.

Act As God/ summoning the lord
I am giddy.

Full of energy because I know what is happening.

I am inspired by the very moment.

This time we act out as god.

In this time together,
summoning the lord.

Fight Alongside God
I work to ensure there is no doom.

No self destruction.

Steering away from the insanity,
the dangerous and the ignorant.

I've written myself in the front lines of the mindful war.

What else is there,
but to write,
and to fight with god?

The Verge of Peace
Wake to technology and intelligence;

Low.

Watch it grow and take over,

live long enough for it to become part of me.

Wake to weapons and war.

The verging mindset of peace and revelation.

Into Heaven
Blood,
back to original hertz.

The heartbeat,
regulated.

Pulling us out of the pits of panic,
calming,
settling our nerves.

And be assured
we have made it into heaven.

The Good Deed
The good deed goes a long way.

A little help turns to smiles,

and smiles, to god.

Fruitful Harvest
I share with my neighbors,
family, friends, and the world
all that has sprung up this year.

At the end of the summer,
an offering.

A happy harvest.

Everyone is smiling.

Enjoying peppers and tea.

Flowers of every colour.

I give them all,
the universe.

Regular Men
Everywhere I go,
easy it is to point out those late to the awakening.

I give them what they need.

Poetic words that would inspire anyone into deep thinking.

Blessed Day
God holds the door open for me.

I ate,
I am loved,
I am healthy.

I am alive and kicking.

Every day is a blessed day.

Proof that I Exist
I am the most dangerous man
because I have nothing.

Nothing left,
but to forgive,

to awaken

invent,

make peace.

The proof of my existence.

Evolution of the Universe
I evolve;

From the mindless animal,

to man, the genius,
the saint
the savior.

Servant to served.

From god, to lord.

Portrait of the Lord
It will be understood
when the world takes up the art.

The angels in heaven paint a picture.

Thickened with colours,

portraits of me,

the lord.

God Deems Me Worthy/ the inevitable character
What is created is what is needed.

What is happening,
is necessary.

My character,
the wackiness,
the emotions.

God,
deemed me worthy.

Oh, No! I Am the Lord!/ the lamb/ shepherd
It is I,
the whole time.

The savior.

The truth seeker,
the speaker.

I am the lord.

The Lamb.

God as my shepherd.

In Tears Finding God
I have enjoyed the show and revelation.

All this fun.

I have been discovered.

The mental game is over.

In tears finding god.

We will play again.

ENERGY
All
ATOM-UNIVERSE/MIND/EXISTENCE
(Earth)
ILLUSION
Radiation
Magnetism
Repulsion
Acceleration
Evaporation
Rain
Heat/motion
Vibration
(Water)
SPACE
Black Hole
MATTER
Potential
Hydrogen
Metal
Torus Field
Space (Air)
Atmos
Water
Life
Mantle
Core
(Fire)
You Are Here
Electric
Dielectric
STARS
137.5077
Empty Space
Light
Separation
Chaos
Weight
Time
Death
Direction
Size
Induction
Capacitance
Discharge
Resistance

Pure Consciousness

WAKING

ANGELS

LORD

INNOCENCE

Guiding Poetry to a Higher Consciousness Series

The BEAUTY of YOUR EXISTENCE

REALITY

HEAVEN

GOD of WRITING

CONSCIOUS

INSANITY

UNIVERSE

REVELATION

INVENTION

RESURRECTION

SURRENDER

INFINITY

Made in the USA
Coppell, TX
19 March 2025

47239043R10098